Walking on the Moon
The Amazing Apollo 11 Mission

Carl R. Green

Enslow Publishers, Inc.
40 Industrial Road
Box 398
Berkeley Heights, NJ 07922
USA

http://www.enslow.com

Original edition published as *Apollo 11 Rockets to First Moon Landing* in 2004.

Library of Congress Cataloging-in-Publication Data

Green, Carl R.
  Walking on the moon : the amazing Apollo 11 mission / Carl R. Green.
      p. cm. — (American space missions-astronauts, exploration, and discovery)
   Includes bibliographical references and index.
   Summary: "Explores the Apollo 11 mission, including the beginning of the Apollo program, the astronauts who made the
journey to the moon, the technology that made it possible, and the historic moon landing"—Provided by publisher.
   ISBN 978-0-7660-4076-2
   1. Project Apollo (U.S.)—Juvenile literature. 2. Apollo 11 (Spacecraft)—Juvenile literature. 3. Spaceflight to the moon—
Juvenile literature. I. Title.
   TL789.8.U6A5354636 2012
   629.45'4—dc23
                              2011037672
Future editions:
Paperback ISBN 978-1-4644-0075-9
ePUB ISBN 978-1-4645-0982-7
PDF ISBN 978-1-4646-0982-4

Printed in the United States of America
032012 Lake Book Manufacturing, Inc., Melrose Park, IL
10 9 8 7 6 5 4 3 2 1

To Our Readers: We have done our best to make sure all Internet addresses in this book were active and appropriate when we went to press. However, the author and the publisher have no control over and assume no liability for the material available on those Internet sites or on other Web sites they may link to. Any comments or suggestions can be sent by e-mail to comments@enslow.com or to the address on the back cover.

♻ Enslow Publishers, Inc., is committed to printing our books on recycled paper. The paper in every book contains 10% to 30% post-consumer waste (PCW). The cover board on the outside of each book contains 100% PCW. Our goal is to do our part to help young people and the environment too!

Illustration Credits: AP Images, p. 13; NASA Headquarters, pp. 4, 10, 25, 38; NASA Johnson Space Center, pp. 1, 6, 18, 26, 29, 33, 36, 41, 42; NASA Kennedy Space Center, pp. 9, 22; NASA Marshall Space Flight Center, pp. 15, 30; SSPL via Getty Images, p. 16; Time & Life Pictures / Getty Images, p. 34.

Cover Illustration: NASA Headquarters (Astronaut Buzz Aldrin saluting the American flag on the Moon).

Contents

One Small Step

On July 16, 1969, a Saturn V rocket blasted skyward from the Kennedy Space Center in Florida. Astronauts Neil Armstrong, Buzz Aldrin, and Michael Collins were tucked into a capsule high atop the giant rocket. Ten years earlier, a Soviet cosmonaut had made headlines by flying in Earth orbit. Now, the American space program was aiming far higher. *Apollo 11* was on its way to the Moon.

The launch went off like clockwork. Eleven minutes later, when *Apollo* reached Earth orbit, a check showed that all systems were "go." The next big moment came when the ship reached the proper point in its orbit. The rocket's third stage fired and kicked the astronauts moonward. Ahead lay a 238,000-mile (382,942-kilometer) journey.

A Trailblazing Adventure

Over the next three days, *Apollo 11* left Earth far behind. Ahead loomed the dark orb of the Moon, backlit at times by a bright halo of sunlight.

Collins fired the service module rocket, slowing *Apollo 11* to 3,600 miles (5,792 kilometers) per hour. Captured by the Moon's gravity, the spaceship settled into lunar orbit. "The view of the Moon . . . is really spectacular," Armstrong said. "It's a view worth the price of the trip."[1]

Leaving Collins to pilot the command module *Columbia,* Armstrong and Aldrin crawled into the lunar module. *Eagle*'s inside paneling had been stripped away. The design saved weight but exposed a jumbled

Eagle, the *Apollo 11* lunar module, is photographed from *Columbia* in its landing configuration during lunar orbit.

mass of wires and pipes. As Aldrin put it, the lander was "about as charming as the cab of a diesel locomotive."[2] After the central command in Houston gave the mission a "go," Collins released the lunar module. "The *Eagle* has wings!" Armstrong exclaimed as the clumsy-looking lander floated free.[3]

While the world waited, spellbound, *Eagle* started its descent. All seemed well until a warning light flashed on the control console. Back on Earth, engineers pinpointed an overworked computer. Guidance officer Stephen Bales studied the report and told Armstrong to keep going. A second alarm sounded minutes later. Again, Bales said there was no need to abort.[4] At this point, *Eagle* hovered just 500 feet (152 meters) above the surface.

The Sea of Tranquility

Armstrong took one look at the programmed landing site and shook his head. *Eagle* was headed toward a crater littered with large boulders. Setting down there would almost surely wreck the module. Armstrong took over the controls and searched for a safer spot to land.

Houston broke in to sound a new warning: "Sixty seconds!" *Eagle* was running low on fuel. If they did not land quickly, the astronauts would be forced to abort the landing. *Eagle's* design did not allow them to tap into the fuel reserved for their ascent.

Long months of training had prepared the crew for this moment. Armstrong grasped the joystick and steered *Eagle* toward a smoother landing zone. As Aldrin called out speed and distance, he flew lower.

Now they were in the "dead man's zone." If they ran out of fuel here, they would crash before they could fire up the ascent engine. At 40 feet (12 meters), *Eagle* began kicking up dust that had not been disturbed for a billion years.[5]

A moment later, *Eagle* settled gently onto the Sea of Tranquility. As Aldrin took his first good look at the bleak moonscape, Armstrong relayed the news to Mission Control. "Houston," he called, "Tranquility Base here. The *Eagle* has landed."[6]

First Man on the Moon

Mission Control checked the data flowing in from *Eagle*'s sensors. If the soil had been too soft, Armstrong would have been told to take off at once. The data, however, showed that the footing was solid. *Eagle* was down safely. With the tension broken, the crew took a well-earned break. Aldrin began by asking his audience on Earth to join him in a brief religious observance. Next came the first meal ever eaten on the Moon. The menu featured bacon squares, sugar cookies, peaches, juice, and coffee.[7]

Their rest break over, the astronauts turned to the task at hand. Piece by piece, they checked out and donned their moonwalk gear. When Armstrong stepped out of the hatch, he was sealed inside a shiny white space suit. A life-support system was strapped to his back. On Earth, he would have tipped the scales at 380 pounds (172.4 kilograms). On the Moon, with a gravity one sixth that of Earth, he weighed just 60 pounds (27.2 kilograms).[8]

Neil Armstrong guided the *Eagle* to a smooth landing on the Sea of Tranquility. In this photo, Buzz Aldrin removes equipment from the lunar module that the two astronauts will use for their scientific experiments.

Neil Armstrong took the first step on the Moon at 10:56 P.M. as millions watched on television. This is one of the footprints that Buzz Aldrin left on the lunar surface.

At 10:56 P.M., Neil Armstrong earned a special place in history. As a television camera whirred, the command pilot stepped onto the Moon. On Earth, millions of people heard him speak the line he had written for this moment. "That's one small step for man," he said, "one giant leap for mankind."[9]

CHAPTER 2

Fulfilling a Solemn Pledge

Apollo 11's **"giant leap"** was much more than a scientific triumph. The United States and the Soviet Union were locked in a long-running struggle known as the Cold War. Each nation viewed the other as a threat to its way of life. The United States believed in democracy and capitalism. The Soviet Union embraced communism and a government that ruled with an iron fist. In the arms race, both countries were building up powerful strike forces. Each had a force of nuclear-tipped missiles aimed at the other's cities.

The Cold War also spawned a more peaceful rivalry known as the space race. Eager to jump out in front, the Soviets assigned their best scientists to their program. The effort paid off with the launch of the first Earth satellite in 1957. In 1961, the gap widened even more when cosmonaut Yuri Gagarin became the first man to fly in Earth orbit.

The American space program, forced to play catch-up, suffered a series of costly rocket mishaps. Stung by the failures, President John F. Kennedy decided that something had to be done—and soon.

The Moon, Kennedy's advisers told him, was the big prize. Once an astronaut planted the Stars and Stripes on the Moon, they said, nothing else would matter.[1] The president agreed. On May 25, 1961, he spoke to Congress about "urgent national needs." Winning the space race is vital, he said, if "we are going to win the battle . . . between freedom and tyranny." Kennedy called on the nation to "commit itself to achieving the goal, before this decade is out, of landing a man on the Moon and returning him safely to Earth."[2]

The words struck a spark. Did the Soviets have a head start? That just made the race more exciting. Would the project cost billions of dollars? Not to worry—consumers spent that much on cigarettes and alcohol each year. Americans had once tamed an unknown continent. Now it was time to explore our nearest neighbor in space.

Gearing Up for a Moon Flight

The task of putting a man on the Moon fell to the National Aeronautics and Space Administration (NASA). On the day Kennedy spoke, NASA's astronauts had logged only fifteen minutes in space. John Glenn's ride to fame as the first American to orbit the Earth was ten months away. Rockets powerful enough to send a manned spaceship to the Moon were still on the drawing boards. Undaunted, NASA began work on a plan called the *Apollo* project.

President John F. Kennedy said winning the space race was "vital" to the United States. He believed that the race could be won by successfully landing men on the Moon. This closeup photo of the Moon was taken by *Apollo 8* astronauts in December 1968.

The challenge was to build a spacecraft that could fly three astronauts to the Moon and back. The return trip was the big question mark. Somehow, the lander would have to carry enough fuel to take off from the Moon and make it back to Earth. The answer, the engineers decided, was to "ferry" two of the astronauts to the Moon's surface. Later, they would fly their lunar module back to the orbiting mother ship for the ride home. This meant that the ships must rendezvous and dock in space. Learning how to perform that maneuver was assigned to the fledgling *Gemini* project.[3]

A crash program gave life to *Apollo*'s four components. Rocket experts built a giant Saturn V booster to provide the thrust. The spacecraft itself was designed in three modules. First came the cone-shaped command module (CM). Three astronauts would ride the CM into space and back to Earth. Next came the service module (SM). The SM would carry fuel, oxygen, electric generators, and its own rocket engine. Firing that engine would provide the thrust for the CM's return trip. Finally, the lunar module (LM) would travel into space inside the Saturn V's third stage. Once Moon orbit was achieved, the CM would retrieve the LM. Two astronauts then would fly it to the lunar surface and back.

To succeed, *Apollo* had to work flawlessly. Once in Earth orbit, the burn that would take *Apollo* to the Moon had to be timed perfectly. An even greater danger would come when the spacecraft slowed to drop into Moon orbit. If the maneuver failed, the astronauts would fly on into deep space, never to return.[4] The LM also had to perform equally well. A rocket failure during descent or ascent would doom the two moonwalkers.

A Rocky Start for Apollo

While engineers designed *Apollo*'s hardware, NASA picked the astronauts who would fly the spacecraft. Most were former test pilots, drawn by the challenge of flying the most complex vehicle ever built. During training, they spent much of their time in simulated spaceflights. The *Apollo 11* team of Neil Armstrong, Buzz Aldrin, and Michael Collins logged two thousand hours in simulators. Actual flights in a lunar lander added realism—and real danger. During one training flight,

Armstrong's lunar lander exploded in a ball of fire. The quick-thinking pilot survived by triggering his ejection seat.[5]

The training covered every aspect of a moon flight. High-speed dives in Air Force transports gave the crews a brief sensation of zero gravity. Strapped sideways in a special rig, the men practiced "walking" in reduced gravity. Each week brought a new lesson. In the classroom, the astronauts learned the basics of Moon geology. Later, they were dropped off in the desert to practice survival skills. Learning to work in

The Saturn V rocket provided the necessary thrust to launch the *Apollo* **spacecraft into space. This photo shows the giant first stage of the Saturn V rocket at a NASA assembly facility.**

Neil Armstrong and Buzz Aldrin, wearing pressurized space suits, practice their lunar surface activities at the Johnson Space Center in Houston, Texas. The *Apollo* astronauts went through months of vigorous training as they prepared for their missions.

space suits turned into an endurance test. Wearing the bulky gear, they said, was like being inside a balloon.[6]

As 1967 dawned, *Apollo* was ready for its first flight. On January 27, Gus Grissom, Ed White, and Roger Chaffee strapped themselves into the *Apollo 1* capsule. The task that day was to rehearse the launch countdown. Suddenly, Chaffee's voice sounded on the intercom. "We've got a fire in the cockpit," he called. Moments later, controllers heard him scream, "We're burning up!" By the time rescue crews pried open the hatch, all three men were dead.[7]

As the nation mourned, NASA went back to the drawing board. Inspectors tore two *Apollo* capsules apart. They found a number of design faults and instances of shoddy workmanship. In the months that followed, engineers made over a thousand changes. Three unmanned flights in 1967 and 1968 proved that the fixes were working. The real test came in October 1968, when *Apollo 7* carried its crew into Earth orbit. The flight ended two days later in a safe splashdown. Everyone at NASA breathed a sigh of relief.

In December 1968, *Apollo 8* flew to the Moon and back. Two flights later, the *Apollo 10* astronauts flew their LM to within 50,000 feet (15.2 kilometers) of the surface. That success put *Apollo 11* in line to make the first Moon landing.

Neil Armstrong

The *Apollo 11* crewmen seemed born to fly the Moon mission. Mission commander Neil Armstrong was a quiet man with superb piloting skills.

Neil Armstrong (left), Michael Collins (center), and Buzz Aldrin posed for this portrait prior to the launch of *Apollo 11*. All three were skilled pilots who were known for quick thinking and staying cool under stress.

No one, it seemed, had ever seen him get rattled. After flying in combat during the Korean War, the Ohio native worked as a test pilot. Flying in *Gemini* 8, his piloting skills saved his out-of-control capsule from almost certain disaster. On Moon landings, the mission commander was posted next to the hatch. That station gave Armstrong the honor of being the first man to set foot on the Moon.

Buzz Aldrin

Flying beside Armstrong was lunar module pilot Edwin "Buzz" Aldrin. Born in New Jersey, the West Point graduate was a brainy problem solver. After flying combat missions in Korea, he went on to earn a doctorate in aeronautics. A high point in his life came when he joined the astronaut corps. During his 1966 flight in *Gemini 12*, he set a record (later broken) for the longest spacewalk. In later years, people often spoke of Aldrin as "the second man on the Moon." When that happened, he would smile and say, "We both landed at the same time."[8]

Michael Collins

The third seat in *Apollo 11* went to command module pilot Michael Collins. While Armstrong and Aldrin landed on the Moon, Collins would fly the CM as it orbited in space. Born in Italy, he attended West Point and went on to a career as an Air Force test pilot. As pilot on *Gemini 10*, he had honed his skills at docking maneuvers. During one of his two spacewalks, he had straddled a rocket stage and ridden it like a cowboy. During training, reporters asked him how he felt about missing the moonwalk. Collins smiled and shook his head. "I'm going ninety-nine and nine-tenths percent of the way there, and that suits me just fine," he said.[9]

CHAPTER 3

Destination: Moon

The crowds gathered near Florida's Cape Kennedy long before dawn on July 16, 1969. By the time the *Apollo 11* crew had eaten a steak-and-eggs breakfast, half a million people were on hand. Millions more turned on their television sets to watch the launch. Neil Armstrong, Buzz Aldrin, and Michael Collins were going to the Moon. No one wanted to miss this historic moment.

Behind the scenes, flight controllers hunched over their computers. Every calculation and every setting had to be double-checked. On the launchpad, workers pumped propellant into the Saturn V's huge tanks. Given the same amount of fuel, a light truck could have driven around the world four hundred times.[1] Inside *Columbia* (the crew's name for the command module), technicians checked banks of instruments, switches, and signal lights. Only two glitches showed up—a leaky valve and a faulty warning light. Both were quickly repaired.[2]

The space-suited astronauts strapped themselves into their seats. A final check showed that all systems were "go." Almost exactly on time,

Saturn's five first-stage engines roared to life. Slowly at first, and then faster and faster, *Apollo* rose into the morning sky. The Moon mission was on its way.

A Textbook Flight

With Collins at the controls, *Apollo* settled into a low Earth orbit. Saturn's first two stages dropped away, leaving stage three to propel the spacecraft moonward. After running a last series of checks, Collins restarted the stage-three engine. A six-minute burn put *Apollo* on a course that would intercept the Moon as it circled the earth. When he reached an escape velocity of 25,000 miles (40,225 kilometers) per hour, Collins detached the stage-three booster. Then he turned the ship and extracted the lunar module, *Eagle,* from the booster. With *Eagle* safely docked, the crew settled in for the three-day flight.[3]

The next job was to put *Apollo* into a "barbecue roll." This slow spin would prevent the sun from frying the ship's electronics on the side exposed to its rays. Their work caught up for the moment, the astronauts stripped off their space suits. At supper time, they used a hot-water gun to prepare a meal of chicken salad, applesauce, and freeze-dried shrimp cocktail. Then they shaded the capsule's windows, dimmed the lights, and stretched out in sleeping bags.[4]

The hours passed quickly. Two days into the flight, Armstrong and Aldrin crawled into the lunar module. *Eagle*'s tiny cabin, they said, was about as big as two phone booths. Both men smelled burned wiring; however, their instruments showed that all was well. The inspection

The Saturn V rocket booster ignites, launching *Apollo 11* skyward on the first leg of its flight to the Moon.

completed, the men returned to *Columbia*. The time for lunar orbit insertion (LOI) was approaching.

On July 19, the order to go for LOI came through. As *Apollo* slipped behind the Moon, Collins fired the engine that reduced the shuttle's speed. The goal was to allow the spacecraft to be captured by the Moon's gravity. If the maneuver failed, *Apollo* might never see Earth again. Those worries faded as the six-minute burn did its job. When Mission Control in Houston asked for a report, Collins was all smiles. "It was like . . . it was perfect," he said.[5]

"A Fine-Looking Machine"

As *Apollo 11* glided around the Moon, the astronauts returned to *Eagle* to continue their preparations. More checklists followed as the pilots flipped switches and exchanged data. After sealing the hatches, Collins received a thumbs-up from Houston. "You are go for separation, *Columbia*," Mission Control said.[6]

A moment later, *Columbia* backed away with a loud thump. As *Eagle* floated free, Armstrong and Aldrin stood side by side at the controls. Elastic cords tethered them to the tiny deck. Sixty miles (97 kilometers) below, the scarred face of the Moon floated past. With more checklists to run through, the astronauts had little time to admire the view. In *Columbia*, Collins stayed in contact. "I think you've got a fine-looking machine there, *Eagle*, despite the fact that you're upside down," he said.[7]

When all was ready, Armstrong fired *Eagle*'s descent engine. The lander moved closer and closer to the Moon as its speed dropped. With the Moon looming ever larger, the computer manuevered *Eagle* into landing position.

Now the astronauts were only 300 feet (91 meters) above the surface. Their speed slowed to just 30 miles (48 kilometers) per hour. When Armstrong saw that *Eagle* was headed toward a boulder-filled crater, he switched off the computer. Pulling back on the joystick, he skimmed over the dangerous crater. Then, with only thirty seconds of fuel left, he found a safer landing zone. As dust billowed in thick clouds, *Eagle* settled safely onto the Moon.[8]

In Houston, the controllers shouted with glee. "Roger. Tranquility, we copy you on the ground," the capsule communicator (CapCom) told the astronauts. "You got a bunch of guys about to turn blue. . . . Thanks a lot."[9]

A Pledge Fulfilled

After attaching a television camera to the lander, Neil Armstrong took his "small step" into history. No one worried that he had meant to say, "That's one small step for a man, one giant leap for mankind." The moment was too exciting to worry about grammar. With only five months left in the decade, NASA had fulfilled the first half of former president Kennedy's pledge.

The first moonwalker pulled down his visor to cut the glare as he stepped out of *Eagle*'s shadow. High above floated the blue sphere of Earth. From this desert moonscape, it looked small and distant. "[The lunar surface] has a stark beauty all its own," Armstrong told a watching world. "It's different, but it's very pretty out here."[10]

Aldrin jumped down to the dusty plain nineteen minutes later. He closed the hatch as he left the lander but was careful not to lock it. Armstrong slapped his friend on the shoulder when they met. "Isn't this fun?" he said with a big grin.[11]

Then it was time to go to work. There were photos to snap, gear to unpack, and experiments to set up. While Armstrong explored a nearby crater, Aldrin snapped open the solar wind panel. That job done, he practiced walking in the light gravity. Each step scattered small sprays of

Neil Armstrong snapped this picture of Buzz Aldrin as his partner explored the Moon's dusty surface.

One of the moonwalking astronauts' main tasks was to conduct experiments. In this photo, Buzz Aldrin has just deployed the solar wind panel (left).

fine-grained lunar soil. Weighing only 60 pounds (27 kilograms) made it easy to move, but hard to stop. Aldrin found that he had to plan ahead several steps if he wanted to stop or turn without falling. Hopping and jumping, he said, made him feel as though he was floating.[12]

Their work done for the moment, the astronauts returned to the lander. A television camera captured the moment as Armstrong unveiled the plaque attached to one of *Eagle*'s landing pads. Signed by President Richard Nixon and the three *Apollo 11* astronauts, it read:

HERE MEN FROM THE PLANET EARTH
FIRST SET FOOT UPON THE MOON
JULY 1969, A.D.
WE CAME IN PEACE FOR ALL MANKIND[13]

To complete the ceremony, the astronauts set up an American flag. Hammer as they might, the pole would not penetrate deeper than eight inches (twenty centimeters). Armstrong used his camera to snap a photo of Aldrin as he saluted the flag. A moment later, CapCom called to say that President Nixon wanted to talk to them. It was, NASA said later, the "longest long-distance phone call" ever made.[14]

"For one priceless moment . . . all the people on this Earth are truly one," Nixon said on the phone. "One in their pride in what you have done. And one in our prayers, that you will return safely to Earth."[15]

"Thank you, Mr. President. . . . It's an honor for us to be able to participate here today," Armstrong replied.[16]

With that, the moonwalkers hurried back to the important tasks that awaited them.

CHAPTER 4

"Task Accomplished"

One of the moonwalkers' roles was to serve as the eyes of scientists back on Earth. Geologists, they knew, were eager to study samples taken from the Moon's surface. To fill their orders, the astronauts collected 48 pounds (21.8 kilograms) of rocks and soil. They chose carefully, gathering specimens of varied sizes and colors. Aldrin, looking for the unusual, picked up some sparkly purple rocks.[1]

The moonwalkers set up an array of scientific gear. The seismic experiment measured lunar quakes and meteor strikes. The data was radioed to Earth and allowed researchers to study the inner structure of the Moon. The device began to pick up the tiny tremors caused by the astronaut's footfalls almost at once. A second device, the laser reflector, bounced laser beams from Earth back to their source. Measuring the beam's travel time allowed scientists to measure the Moon's exact distance from Earth. The solar wind panel trapped atomic particles

Buzz Aldrin completes the set up for the seismic experiment on the lunar surface. The sensitive equipment relayed data to Earth that allowed researchers to study the inner structure of the Moon.

streaming from the sun. The particles, researchers hoped, would help them understand the nature of solar radiation.[2]

The televised images streaming back to Earth showed two ghostly, space-suited figures. Helmets shielded the astronauts from the sun's glare. Life-support backpacks supplied them with oxygen. Temperature-control systems insulated them from the deadly cold and broiling heat. Layer upon layer of tough fabric guarded against leaks. A moonwalker who ripped his suit on a sharp rock would be dead in seconds.

As the clock ticked, Mission Control carefully monitored the astronauts' heart rates. Pleased by the readings, controllers added thirty

Buzz Aldrin (left), Michael Collins (center), and Neil Armstrong present Frank Taylor, president of the Smithsonian Institute, with a Moon rock. Geologists were anxious to study the soil and rock samples that Armstrong and Aldrin collected on the Moon.

minutes to the moonwalk. Finally, at the two-and-a-half hour mark, they gave the order to leave.[3] Before closing the hatch, Armstrong and Aldrin tossed a small packet onto the ground near the lander. Inside the packet was a goodwill message, a gold olive branch, an *Apollo 1* patch, and two medals. The patch and the medals honored the three astronauts and two cosmonauts who had given their lives to the quest to explore space.[4]

No Second Chances

Back in the lander, the astronauts prepared for the ascent. To save weight, they dumped their excess gear outside the lander. With the hatch sealed and their helmets off, they sniffed the sharp, ashy odor of moon dust for the first time. Aldrin thought it smelled like gunpowder.[5] After Houston quizzed them about the moonwalk, the two men settled down to rest. Sleep did not come easily in the cramped, chilly cabin. Earthlight flooding through the windows made it even more difficult for Armstrong to sleep.

While the astronauts slept, instruments detected a sharp impact on the lunar surface. The Soviets, in an effort to steal *Apollo 11*'s glory, had tried to land an unmanned spacecraft. If *Luna 15* had scooped up some soil and beaten *Apollo* back to Earth, the gamble might have paid off. *Apollo 11*'s luck was still good, however. Instead of a soft landing, the Soviet spacecraft crashed a few hundred miles away.[6]

Eagle's next test was to make a proper ascent. The astronauts knew they had one chance to get it right. High overhead, orbiting in *Columbia*, Michael Collins knew it, too. If something went wrong, he would be forced to return to Earth alone. The thought filled him with dread.[7]

In the end, the ascent was trouble free. The engine fired on schedule, leaving the descent stage behind as it rocketed *Eagle* skyward. Once the ascent stage reached orbit, a series of short burns moved it in close to *Columbia*.

In the command module, Collins used his thrusters to close the gap. The two ships docked with hardly a bump. Moments later, as Collins put it, "All hell broke loose."[8] One of *Eagle*'s thrusters fired briefly, throwing the ships into a jerking spin. Reacting quickly, Collins used his own thrusters to regain control. The danger past, the moonwalkers took a moment to vacuum moon dust off their suits. Then they handed the sealed rock boxes through to Collins. "I handled them," he said later, "as if they were . . . jam-packed with rare jewels."[9]

Armstrong and Aldrin crawled back to their seats in *Columbia*. With the hatches closed, Collins cut *Eagle* loose to drift in Moon orbit. The three men relaxed for a while and then turned to the job of preparing for the return to Earth. Collins fired the three-minute "get-us-home burn" while *Columbia* was behind the Moon. Ten minutes later, the ship flew back into radio contact with Earth.

"How did it go? Over," CapCom Charlie Duke asked from Houston. When Michael Collins confirmed that all was well, Duke relaxed. "Roger," he said. "We got you coming home."[10]

Splashdown in the Pacific

The long downhill "coast" to Earth took nearly three days. Thanks to Houston's precise programming, only one small midcourse correction was needed. Collins left the controls long enough to prepare his favorite space lunch of cream of chicken soup.[11] Along with some chores, the crew slept, listened to music, and caught up on news from home.

As the hours counted down, the astronauts cut loose the service module. With *Columbia* moving at thirty times the speed of sound, the reentry angle had to be perfect. If the angle were too steep, the capsule

Soon after their successful splashdown, the *Apollo 11* astronauts left *Columbia* and climbed into a life raft. A Navy diver joined them as they waited to be picked up by a helicopter from the **USS Hornet**.

would burn up when it hit the atmosphere. If it were too shallow, the spacecraft would skip off into space. Once again, the numbers were right on target. The astronauts watched their heat shield glow a fiery orange-yellow as the ship plunged into the atmosphere. Lookouts on the USS *Hornet* saw what looked like a meteor streaking across the sky.

Joan Aldrin (center), Buzz's wife, leads the applause as family and friends celebrate *Apollo 11*'s successful splashdown.

Drogue chutes popped out to steady the speeding capsule. Moments later, the three main parachutes opened with a comforting jerk. Slowed to 21 miles (34 kilometers) per hour, *Columbia* splashed into the Pacific Ocean—and promptly turned upside down. Working swiftly, the men inflated a set of air bags that turned the capsule right side up. By that time, a rescue team dispatched from the USS *Hornet* had reached them. Before they opened the hatch, the astronauts swallowed motion-sickness pills. This was no time to get seasick.

In the control room in Houston, a big message board lit up. First, the main panel spelled out President Kennedy's 1961 pledge to land a man on the Moon and return him safely to Earth. Then a side panel lit up with this proud announcement:

TASK ACCOMPLISHED

JULY 1969[12]

Heroes in Quarantine

The *Apollo* crew returned to cheers and banner headlines, but not to hugs and handshakes. Some officials were worried that the astronauts might have carried alien germs back to Earth. The director of the lunar receiving lab said he did not expect to find any harmful life-forms. "But," he added, "you can't be too careful."[13] The moment the astronauts opened the hatch, a Navy diver handed them a set of isolation suits. After climbing into a life raft, they sprayed each other with disinfectant. The waiting sailors gave the capsule the same treatment.

Back at the *Hornet*, the space heroes were hustled into a mobile quarantine unit. Once inside, the astronauts peeled off their sweaty suits and took long showers. Refreshed and dressed in flying outfits, they looked out to see President Nixon waiting to welcome them.[14] Three days later, the unit was flown back to Texas and trucked to an $8 million quarantine facility. A team of doctors and technicians showed the crew their quarters and started medical tests. Far underground, a second team broke open the first box of moon rocks.

Neil Armstrong (left), Michael Collins (center), and Buzz Aldrin look out the window of their mobile quarantine facility as they talk to President Richard Nixon. The three astronauts had to endure days of medical testing before the quarantine was lifted.

Eighteen days after splashdown, the lab gave each of the astronauts a clean bill of health. Neither the men nor the moon rocks were hosts to alien life-forms. The lab director broke the quarantine seal, and the space heroes stepped into the glare of television lights. It was the first step in a long victory lap.

CHAPTER 5

Out of the Cradle

***Apollo 11* vaulted the United States** into the lead in the space race. The triumph of American know-how inspired a wave of national pride. Even so, thoughtful people knew that the Moon landing belonged to all people and all nations. Back in the 1930s, Konstantin Tsiolkovsky had dreamed about spaceflight. "Earth is the cradle of mankind," the Soviet rocket scientist wrote. "But you cannot live in the cradle forever."[1]

Driven by a thirst for knowledge and adventure, a new wave of pioneers had ventured skyward. Tsiolkovsky would have been the first to applaud their feat. At long last, he might have said, humanity had left the cradle.

A Whirlwind Tour

As the quarantine ended, the nation embraced the *Apollo 11* crew. For a time, Americans forgot that they were fighting a costly war in Vietnam.

The *Apollo 11* astronauts wave to an enormous crowd as they ride through New York City in the back of a convertible. The ticker-tape parade was only one of many similar celebrations.

President Nixon led the salutes. United by "the Spirit of Apollo," he said, the country had shown that it could solve any problem.[2]

Messages poured into Houston from around the globe. Some came from high places. Pope Paul VI and the king of Belgium sent admiring best wishes. Other notes came from the streets. The Camel Drivers Radio Club of Afghanistan welcomed the *Apollo 11* astronauts as honorary members. The mailbox also overflowed with invitations.

Michael Collins laughed when he was asked to attend a rodeo. "Anyone that can ride that whatever-it-is the way you did has gotta be a darn good cowboy," the letter said.[3]

In a blur of busy days, August 13 stood out. In the morning, New York City treated the astronauts to a ticker-tape parade. Next came a flight to Chicago for a reception and a round of speeches. The day ended in Los Angeles, at a state dinner hosted by President Nixon. A month later, the astronauts and their families took off on a seven-week trip through twenty-five countries. As cheering crowds looked on, the heroes shook hands with dozens of world leaders.[4]

Nothing in their training had prepared the astronauts for this sudden brush with fame. Even so, each met the test with patience and good humor. It was a bumpy ride at times, but the three men seemed to enjoy the once-in-a-lifetime experience.[5]

Building on a Space Triumph

The *Apollo* project did not end with *Apollo 11*. *Apollo 12, 14, 15, 16*, and *17* each made a safe landing on the Moon. Only *Apollo 13*, crippled by an explosion, failed to complete its mission. The crew made it back to Earth by using the lunar module as a "lifeboat." In July 1971, the *Apollo 15* moonwalkers climbed into a lunar rover and took the first drive across the Moon. In April 1972, the *Apollo 16* crew completed the first exploration of the highlands of the Moon. From December 11 to 14, 1972, the *Apollo 17* moonwalkers spent a record twenty-two hours exploring the Moon's surface.

The *Apollo 17* flight ended the *Apollo* project. The world's scientists hardly noticed. They were busy studying 838 pounds (380 kilograms) of moon rocks. As the weeks went by, labs around the world announced their findings. Tests showed that some rocks were 4 billion years old, but none contained any sign of life. The rocks did contain elements common to Earth such as iron, silicon, and oxygen. However, the chemical links that bound the elements together differed from those found in Earth rocks. One mineral from *Apollo 11*'s collection turned out to be entirely new. Scientists named the titanium-rich compound armalcolite. The name honored the crew: *arm-* for Armstrong, *-al-* for Aldrin, *-col-* for Collins.[6]

As the headlines faded, the *Apollo 11* astronauts went on to new challenges. After leaving NASA, Michael Collins worked for the State Department. A year later, he moved up to the top job at the National Air and Space Museum. After a brief tour of duty with the Air Force, Buzz Aldrin ran his own consulting company. NASA, his old boss, hired him to help design the space shuttle. Neil Armstrong went on to teach at the University of Cincinnati. In 1986, he served on the commission that studied the *Challenger* space shuttle disaster.[7]

Lasting Footprints

The race to the Moon united Americans in pursuit of a grand prize. Thousands of people worked together to build and launch the *Apollo* spacecraft. Today, that unity seems lost. The nation is focused on

The *Apollo* program continued until the final moon landing of *Apollo 17*. In this photo, astronaut John W. Young, commander of the *Apollo 16* mission, jumps to salute the American flag. The *Apollo 16* crew completed the first exploration of the Moon's highlands.

tasks such as fighting terrorism and protecting endangered species. Somehow, these challenges seem less inspiring—and less easily solved.

Today's big space project, the International Space Station, attracts few headlines. Perhaps the nation is waiting for the inspiration to stretch even further. Should we gear up for a manned flight to Mars? Whatever comes next, the footprints left in the sands of the Sea of Tranquility will survive. Unless a meteorite strike destroys them, they will be there a million years from now.[8]

Mission specialist John Newman waves at the camera while working outside the International Space Station. Although current space missions may not capture the world's attention like the first Moon landing did in 1969, the United States and countries around the globe are still responding to the challenge of space exploration.

Chapter Notes

Chapter 1. One Small Step

1. Buzz Aldrin and Malcolm McConnell, *Men from Earth* (New York: Bantam Books, 1989), p. 233.

2. Ibid., p. 232.

3. Patrick J. Walsh, *Echoes Among the Stars: A Short History of the U.S. Space Program* (Armonk, N.Y.: M. E. Sharpe, 2000), p. 88.

4. Charles Murray and Catherine Bly Cox, *Apollo: The Race to the Moon* (New York: Simon and Schuster, 1989), pp. 352–353.

5. Aldrin, p. 238.

6. David R. Williams, "30th Anniversary of Apollo 11: 1969–1999," n.d., <http://nssdc.gsfc.nasa.gov/planetary/lunar/Apollo_11_30th.html> (December 5, 2002).

7. Timothy B. Benford and Brian Wilkes, *The Space Program Quiz & Fact Book* (New York: Harper & Row, Publishers, 1985), p. 73.

8. Walsh, p. 90.

9. William Roy Shelton, *Winning the Moon* (Boston: Little, Brown & Co., 1970), p. 174.

Chapter 2. Fulfilling a Solemn Pledge

1. Charles Murray and Catherine Bly Cox, *Apollo: The Race to the Moon* (New York: Simon and Schuster, 1989), p. 79.

2. Buzz Aldrin and Malcolm McConnell, *Men from Earth* (New York: Bantam Books, 1989), p. 68.

3. Wayne Lee, *To Rise from Earth: An Easy-to-Understand Guide to Spaceflight* (New York: Facts on File, Inc., 2000), pp. 125–126.

4. Ibid., p. 130.

5. Patrick J. Walsh, *Echoes Among the Stars: A Short History of the U.S. Space Program* (Armonk, N.Y.: M. E. Sharpe, 2000), pp. 71–72.

6. University of Colorado, "What Does It Take to Go to Space?" n.d., <http://www.cualum.org/heritage/educational_resources/what_take.html> (July 15, 2003).

7. Lee, p. 137.

8. Timothy B. Benford and Brian Wilkes, *The Space Program Quiz & Fact Book* (New York: Harper & Row, Publishers, 1985), p. 114.

9. William Roy Shelton, *Winning the Moon* (Boston: Little, Brown & Co., 1970), p. 160.

Chapter 3. Destination: Moon

1. Sign posted at Virginia Air and Space Center (Hampton, Virginia), May 2003.

2. Al Hall, ed., *Petersen's Book of Man in Space: A Giant Leap for Mankind, vol. 4* (Los Angeles: Petersen Publishing Co., 1974), pp. 128–129.

3. Wayne Lee, *To Rise from Earth: An Easy-to-Understand Guide to Spaceflight* (New York: Facts on File, Inc., 2000), p. 131.

4. Buzz Aldrin and Malcolm McConnell, *Men from Earth* (New York: Bantam Books, 1989), pp. 229–230.

5. Ibid., p. 233.

6. Ibid., p. 234.

7. David R. Williams, "30th Anniversary of Apollo 11: 1969–1999," n.d., <http://nssdc. gsfc.nasa.gov/planetary/lunar/Apollo_11_30th.html> (December 5, 2002).

8. David West Reynolds, *Apollo: The Epic Journey to the Moon* (New York: Harcourt, Inc., 2002), p. 136.

9. Ibid., p. 141.

10. Ibid., p. 146.

11. Aldrin, p. 241.

12. William Roy Shelton, *Winning the Moon* (Boston: Little, Brown & Co., 1970), p. 176.

13. Aldrin, p. 242.

14. Peter Bond, *Heroes in Space: From Gagarin to Challenger* (New York: Basil Blackwell, 1987), p. 200.

15. Shelton, p. 177.

16. Ibid., p. 178.

Chapter 4. "Task Accomplished"

1. Peter Bond, *Heroes in Space: From Gagarin to Challenger* (New York: Basil Blackwell, 1987), pp. 200–201.

2. "Apollo 11 Science Experiments," November 28, 2001, <http://cass.jsc.nasa.gov/ expmoon/Apollo11/A11_science.html> (December 5, 2002).

3. Bond, pp. 201–202.

4. Buzz Aldrin and Malcolm McConnell, *Men from Earth* (New York: Bantam Books, 1989), p. 243.

5. Ibid., p. 244.

6. Patrick J. Walsh, *Echoes Among the Stars: A Short History of the U.S. Space Program* (Armonk, N.Y.: M. E. Sharpe, 2000), p. 92.

7. Bond, p. 203.

8. Michael Collins, *Carrying the Fire: An Astronaut's Journeys* (New York: Farrar, Straus, and Giroux, 1974), p. 416.

9. Bond, p. 205.

10. Ibid., p. 206.

11. Collins, p. 425.

12. Charles Murray and Catherine Bly Cox, *Apollo: The Race to the Moon* (New York: Simon and Schuster, 1989), p. 370.

13. William Roy Shelton, *Winning the Moon* (Boston: Little, Brown & Co., 1970), p. 184.

14. Collins, p. 444.

Chapter 5. Out of the Cradle

1. Quote posted at Virginia Air and Space Center (Hampton, Virginia), May 2003.

2. Timothy B. Benford and Brian Wilkes, *The Space Program Quiz & Fact Book* (New York: Harper & Row, Publishers, 1985), p. 93.

3. Michael Collins, *Carrying the Fire: An Astronaut's Journeys* (New York: Farrar, Straus, and Giroux, 1974), p. 450.

4. Ibid., pp. 455–456.

5. Patrick J. Walsh, *Echoes Among the Stars: A Short History of the U.S. Space Program* (Armonk, N.Y.: M. E. Sharpe, 2000), p. 95.

6. Benford, p. 53.

7. Peter Bond, *Heroes in Space: From Gagarin to Challenger* (New York: Basil Blackwell, 1987), p. 212.

8. David R. Williams, "30th Anniversary of Apollo 11: 1969–1999," n.d., <http://nssdc.gsfc.nasa.gov/planetary/lunar/Apollo_11_30th.html> (December 5, 2002).

Glossary

Apollo—The series of space missions which landed U.S. astronauts on the surface of the Moon.

CapCom—The communications expert who relays information between Mission Control and the flight crew during a space mission.

command module (CM)—The component of the *Apollo* spacecraft that carried three astronauts into orbit around the Moon and later returned them to Earth.

lunar module (LM)—The component of the *Apollo* spacecraft that landed astronauts on the Moon and later flew them back to dock with the command module.

Mission Control—A room filled with computers and communications equipment used by flight controllers to monitor spaceflights.

orbit—The path of one celestial body or artificial satellite around another.

quarantine—The medical practice of holding people or animals in isolation that have been exposed to infectious or contagious diseases.

reentry—The phase of a spaceflight in which astronauts and their spacecraft first encounter the Earth's atmosphere during their return from a mission.

thrusters—An assembly of small rockets used to control the position of a spacecraft.

velocity—The rate of speed of an object as it moves in a given direction.

Further Reading

Books

Chaikin, Andrew, with Victoria Kohl. *Mission Control, This is Apollo: The Story of the First Voyage to the Moon.* New York: Viking, 2009.

Dyer, Alan. *Mission to the Moon.* New York: Simon & Schuster Books for Young Readers, 2009.

Floca, Brian. *Moonshot: The Flight of Apollo 11.* New York: Atheneum Books for Young Readers, 2009.

Godwin, Robert. *First Men on the Moon: Apollo 11.* Burlington, Ont.: Apogee Books, 2006.

Thimmesh, Catherine. *Team Moon: How 400,000 People Landed Apollo 11 on the Moon.* Boston: Houghton Mifflin, 2006.

Internet Addresses

NASA: Apollo 11
   <http://www.nasa.gov/mission_pages/apollo/missions/apollo11.html>

Smithsonian National Air and Space Museum: The Apollo Program
   <http://www.nasm.si.edu/collections/imagery/apollo/as11/a11.htm>

We Choose the Moon: John F. Kennedy Presidential Library & Museum
   <http://wechoosethemoon.org/>

Index

A

Aldrin, Edwin "Buzz," 5–8, 14, 19, 20–24, 27, 28, 30–32, 40

Apollo 1, 17, 30

Apollo 11
  astronaut training, 14–17
  design of, 12–14, 17
  Earth orbit, 5, 21
  flight, 21–22
  honors for astronauts, 37–39
  launch, 20–21
  lunar landing, 7–8, 23–24
  lunar module ascent, 31
  lunar orbit, 5–7, 22
  moonwalk, 8–10, 24–30
  quarantine, 35–36
  return, splashdown, 32–35
  space docking, 13, 19, 21, 31–32

Apollo project, 17, 30, 39–40

armalcolite, 40

Armstrong, Neil, 5–10, 14–15, 17–18, 20–24, 27, 30–32, 40

B

Bales, Stephen, 7

barbecue roll, 21

C

Chaffee, Roger, 17

Cold War, 11

Collins, Michael, 5–8, 14, 19–24, 31–32, 39, 40

Columbia (command module), 6, 13–14, 23–24, 31–35

E

Eagle (lunar module), 6–8, 13–14, 21–24, 31–32

escape velocity, 21

G

Gagarin, Yuri, 5, 11

Gemini project, 13, 18, 19

Glenn, John, 12

goodwill packet, 30

Grissom, Gus, 17

K

Kennedy, John F., 12, 35

L

Luna 15, 31

M

Moon
  first meal on, 8
  rocks, 28–29, 35–36, 40
  study of, 28–29

walking on, 25–27
weight on, 8–10, 27

N

NASA, 12, 14, 17, 24, 27

Nixon, Richard, 27, 35, 38, 39

S

Saturn V rocket, 5, 13–14, 20, 21

Sea of Tranquility, 7–8

Soviet Union, 5, 11–12, 31

space race, 11–12, 24, 31, 37

space suits, 8, 15–17, 21, 29

T

Tranquility Base, 7–8

Tsiolkovsky, Konstantin, 37

U

United States, 11–12

USS *Hornet*, 33–35

W

White, Ed, 17